THE MISSING HANDLE

THE MISSING HANDLE

Finding Meaning When
There Is None
to Be Had

ROBERT J. EISEN

RESOURCE *Publications* · Eugene, Oregon

THE MISSING HANDLE
Finding Meaning When There Is None to Be Had

Resource Publications
An Imprint of Wipf and Stock Publishers
199 W. 8th Ave., Suite 3
Eugene, OR 97401

www.wipfandstock.com

PAPERBACK ISBN: X978-1-6667-5024-9
HARDCOVER ISBN: 978-1-6667-5025-6
EBOOK ISBN: 978-1-6667-5026-3

VERSION NUMBER 121422

An earlier version of the essay concerning *Hadesh Yameinu K'kedem* included in Chapter 5 appeared in the September 22, 2017 issue of *The Arizona Jewish Post*.

Front piece: "It is You...", *The Koren Sacks Siddur, Nusah Sepharad,* Second Hebrew/English Edition, 2013, p. 509, included with the permission of Koren Publishers Jerusalem.

All Bible translations are the work of the author.

Dedicated to the smiley giggles of our granddaughter, Reese, whose presence has enabled me to see the world for what it still can be.

שועת עניים אתה תשמע

It is You who hears the pleading of the poor

צעקת הדל תקשיב ותושיע

You will listen to the cries of the destitute and save them

Contents

Preface

ATTENDED HEBREW UNION COLLEGE – Jewish Institute of Religion (the seminary of the Union for Reform Judaism), joined the Rabbinical Assembly (association of Conservative rabbis) and served Conservative congregations for almost my entire career, walks into an Orthodox *shul* and...

Sounds like the beginning of a bad bar joke: A rabbi, a minister and a priest walk into a bar and... This is a line that I have used many times to quiet down a crowd (people want to hear what happened), only to disappoint them by then starting the program. However, here, I use that line as an introduction because it is the outline of my story and why I am telling it as well.

I often joke (meaning no offense) that I had a "schizophrenic upbringing." Though we were affiliated with a Reform congregation, my fondest and most meaningful memories are from the Orthodox *shul* that we often attended to be with my mother's parents and family. Running between the women's section upstairs and the men's below, clinging to my grandfather's *tzitzit* (tassels on the corners of his *tallit*, prayer shawl) and staring with eager eyes and ears at the *hazan* (cantor) chant the service with such passion, left much more of an impression on me than sitting and listening to the largest pipe organ in the area and a professional non-Jewish choir. That I ended up in the middle (as part of the Conservative movement) was almost to be expected. That history also enables me to tell this story as I am.

This book is not a halakhic work. You will not find a categorized list of *mitzvot* (commandments) described and interpreted as a guide for mourners. Neither is it a systematic theology formalizing how one should embrace their grief. It is a reflection of my own grief and mourning in response to the death of our younger son. It is sometimes very raw. It sometimes pedantic. But, it is my story.

The core of this story is based on a journal I kept during the first year after our son Ricky's death. Writing was my way of processing the ups and downs of my journey through the valley of the shadow of death. And, having the journal as a companion enabled me to be there to listen to my wife and older son. It was a very personal journey, one which dramatically impacted the way in which I engaged with families when a death occurred – especially the second year after Ricky died when I had six funerals over the course of six months, all of which were kids of his age or younger (I had an understanding with the cemetery that when they set up for a funeral, my back was always towards Ricky's grave). I shared a very rough draft on the first anniversary of his death with just a few people (and even fewer of them ever read it!). So why do I share it now?

Mourning is very personal. No two stories are ever exactly the same. And yet, there are some common experiences we all endure. Because of how idiosyncratic grief and mourning can be I have been extremely reluctant to turn this project into something more than a digital file. My wife, however, suggested, when I told her that I was thinking of publishing the story, that if even one person found any degree of solace it would be well worth the effort. So, I share this story hoping that as people do find their place in it here or there, they will find that which will give them a little piece of peace.

One spoiler alert: The subtitle of this book (Finding Meaning When There is None to be Had) might suggest to some that I am going to provide THE answer to such a "question." The truth is that there is not one correct answer. In fact, there are many.

As you will read, the foundation of the journal is a reflection on the moment when, during the course of the funeral, we discovered that the handle needed to lower Ricky into the grave was missing, the actual interment would have to wait. Whether it was forgotten or it was a sign is discussed below. However (one more spoiler alert), in retrospect, I sometimes think that any meaning that might be had when life seems utterly bereft of any at all, can be found in exactly such pauses. When we stop and start to look at the world for what it is, take the time to see the bigger picture, allow our hearts and minds to open themselves up to the wonder of life as it is lived, there is more meaning to be found than in any number of books, or poems or prayers.

Is all of life just a series of coincidences? Is all of life a chaotic crapshoot? Is all of life a series of accidents? When we pause to see what the world still can be, when we look up above the walls of the valley, or at the glimmer of light at the end of its shadow, finding meaning is not only possible, it is probable.

So, what's with my poor attempt at a bar joke? This story sat trapped as a digital file on my hard drive for four years. Until we moved to Phoenix and began to live life anew, I had no intention of doing more than reading it on Ricky's *yahrtzeit* (the anniversary of his death). And then I walked into not one, but two, "bars."

Finding a *shul* in Phoenix was very important to me. Though the pandemic limited the range of my search, I did look for a place that I could call home. I bounced around until I found The New Shul in Scottsdale. There, Rabbis Michael Wasserman and Elana Kanter have created something I had never experienced before. They have given me a renewed passion in and for prayer. Every Shabbat, as I look around the sanctuary, I notice how so many different people find themselves bound together as one through the form of worship. What binds such a disparate group of people into a community? For some, it is the shared history that they have created over the past 20 year. For others, it is in the comradery of just being together with other Jews. For all, I do believe, it is the understanding that for whatever reason we might be there, we are in it together as one: with and for each other; a oneness that the rabbis more than just encourage. That "oneness" encouraged me to pursue the publication of this story. It was a oneness that I desperately needed, and one which I hope this book can provide to those who are on any kind of journey similar to mine (even if it is only one person).

At the same time, I walked into an Orthodox *shul*, Ahavas Torah: The Scottsdale Torah Center, and found Rabbi Ariel Shoshan. Our paths had crossed a couple of times over the years, but we never really connected (in fact, at one encounter I was a little rude to him). Without hesitation, but with the principled integrity to maintain his credibility as an Orthodox rabbi, he invited me in to be a part of his congregation. From what he has created, and the classes into which he has welcomed me, I have experienced "living Judaism" in a manner that has always eluded me. That he accepts me for who I am needs to be acknowledged. When I reflected on the example of the framework of Torah that he embodies, I began to think that even as this work is far from a halakhic guidebook, still, it might offer that one person an insight into how to manage their grief and mourning within the parameters of our tradition.

Throughout this journey I have done more listening than talking with my family. Partly because, strange as it may sound, I find that I say more by listening than talking. That Ricky is not here has left an incredible hole in our hearts. At times we have tried to fill that hole with each other. At times we have just acknowledged that it is there, and that is enough. I have only an undying love and respect for my wife, Debby (I am the lucky one in this relationship), and our son Alex. Carly, Alex's wife got to know Ricky as only Ricky could introduce himself, but stuck around anyway, and for that I will be forever thankful. And now we have Reese, who, sometimes doesn't seem to fully distinguish between play time and nap time, but has made a significant difference in our lives, and given us all a better appreciation for life and love.

As I have reviewed this manuscript so many times I have wondered if it might have been better to share this from a prone position on a couch with a therapist. However, when I paused and looked at the missing handle I thought otherwise.

As I wrote (you will see below):

> *There is no end to the making of books, especially concerning bereavement, pain, suffering and grief. Why am*

I sharing these thoughts as I am? What makes this one so different or special? Because it is mine. This is my story. I offer it with the hope and the prayer that because of it (or maybe in spite of it) you will find your story and find a little piece of peace for yourself as well.

I do not ask for sympathy. I ask that no hardship fall on anyone. I only ask that when faced with mourning, we find a way to make their memories live, for their sake if not for ours.

May we each find our missing handles.

Acknowledgements

I WANT TO EXTEND my most heartfelt appreciation to everyone who helped bring this story to the printed page. Nancy Ben-Asher Ozeri offered commentary and insight that gave a much needed form to the words, sentences and paragraphs. Pastor Glen Elliott, Autumn Wiley-Hill, PhD and Rabbi Perry Raphael Rank each helped me make sense out of what I had written in new and different ways. My wife, Debby, son and daughter-in-law, Alex and Carly, were silent witnesses to the evolution of this printed version of my story, not knowing that I was writing it, but very much influencing its growth. I owe each of them more than they will ever know. And last, but not least, I owe Piper, my grand-dog, an extra few moments sniffing the scenery along our walks and a special treat beyond what she already is able to get from me.

Introduction

HIS LIFE ENDED THE same way that it began, with a phone call.

July 6, 1989. 6:30 am, the phone rang. It was my mother-in-law: "Bob, this is Esther. Don't get excited, but Debby is in the hospital, she has gone into labor."

Don't get excited? Don't worry? What was I supposed to do? And yet, even in that nanosecond when I wanted to scream as loud as I could: "What is going on?" A certain sense of calmness prevailed. I could not help but think that something I would never be able to explain was going on.

I was in Raleigh, NC when the call came. My wife, Debby, was with her parents in Rochester, NY. We had been in Raleigh for three years. We loved the area, and the congregation was wonderful. However, over the course of those three years both my mother-in-law and father-in-law were diagnosed with cancer. A pulpit with a congregation in Buffalo (an hour from Rochester) had opened up and I had just that week learned that I had gotten the job, which would begin August 1. Debby was visiting her parents and we had decided that it was best for her to just stay there. I would pack up the house and arrange the move. Everything seemed to be falling into place. But then I got the phone call. After a very difficult pregnancy (where we thought we might have lost him very early on) Ricky decided it was his time to enter the world . . . two months early.

Why the calm? What was I unable to explain? Coincidentally (or not), I was scheduled to fly up to Rochester that very morning to officiate at a wedding over the weekend. Timing is everything. Over the course of that nanosecond I felt that absolutely nothing was wrong. For some reason, this is the way it is supposed to be. What that reason was, and what I was supposed to learn from it, took 28 years to discover, even as clues appeared over and over again.

The plane landed. Rachel, Debby's older sister, picked me up at the airport. We have very different memories of what happened then. I heard my self asking, very calmly, "What is going on?" She remembers me shouting. What mattered most, however, were the answers: It was a boy: 3 lbs. 5 oz. Debby was OK and resting, after an emergency C-section.

Rachel dropped me off at the hospital and I went directly to Debby's room. It was not in the maternity wing, but in a different area on the same floor. Someone had decided that it would be better, in case Ricky did not make it. When I got to her room, I had to catch my breath. It was the same room that her mother had been in many times over the past two years for her surgeries and treatments.

The first thing she said to me was "Don't cry." I didn't. We talked and I went to see Ricky in the NICU. The doctor just happened to be there. It was someone I knew from when I had been an assistant rabbi in Rochester before moving to Raleigh. Things were not good, but they were not as bad as they could be either. "Time will tell," I was told. The next few days would be critical.

Ricky was a fighter. Within several days he was transferred to a different hospital where he resided in the NICU for six weeks. I went back to Raleigh, closed up the house, moved in with my in-laws and commuted to and from Buffalo as we tried to put a transition plan in place.

On the days that I was in Buffalo, the NICU nurses held his 10:00 pm feeding for me, so when I returned to Rochester I could feed him. The attending pediatrician had no problem with the arrangement; he had been Debby's pediatrician "several years" earlier. I pushed the formula through a syringe and a feeding tube, timed at one cc a minute. And so it was, sustained by ventilators and IVs, in the midst of flashing monitors and the chirping of whirring machines, Ricky came into this world, and he began to teach me lessons that I took too long to learn.

August 20, 2017. 6:30 am, the phone rang. "Dad" (it was our older son), "I just got a call from a friend. Something is wrong with Ricky and he is on his way to the ER at Banner." I got that friend's phone number, and found out that something had happened, the details of which are still a bit hazy. Ricky had had some sort of seizure and heart attack. He had been "out" for some time. The ambulance was taking him to the ER. We dressed as fast as we could.

Upon arriving at the hospital, we were ushered to a room between the ER and the Trauma Center. We were not told much of anything, or even if we could see Ricky. A chaplain walked by hurriedly, asking if we wanted a prayer even as she headed off in a different direction. After a while I went into the ER to try to find out what was going on and if we could see him. We were escorted into the Trauma Unit. They knew who we were and avoided eye contact. I knew that was not good. There were innumerable questions, but few, if any, answers. Part of me felt like the doctors had already "written him off" until we had shown up. They tried to be encouraging, but their body language told a different story.

Ricky was cold when we saw him. His eyes were glazed over, lifeless and staring into some sort of beyond. We were told that there would be a CAT scan and then he would probably be moved upstairs.

The next time we went in to see him he had already been moved. Eventually we found out that he had been taken to the ICU and we were escorted there. There were a few procedures that they would have to do (cool down his body and then warm him back up to assess the degree of any brain damage). And so, it was déjà vu all over again. . . . We sat and watched him sustained by ventilators and IVs, in the midst of flashing monitors and the chirping of whirring machines. We watched for three days.

On August 22 it was determined that there was really nothing that could be done. The brain damage was significant. We were escorted into a room where we met with a representative of the Donor Network of Arizona. How did we feel about organ donation? Debby and I had not spoken about it, but we both said that we wanted to do whatever we could at the same time. The woman we were with smiled. She asked if we knew that Ricky had registered as an organ donor when he got his license. We did not. We proceeded with the interview and on August 23, 2017, at 1:19 am Ricky was pronounced dead and his kidneys were harvested for transplant (which we were informed was successful).

Ricky was buried on the morning of August 24. That day was, as best as we can remember, close to, if not, his original due date. He had rushed into this world and raced out the same way 28 years later.

Anyone who has lost a loved one can empathize with the pain that comes with their death. So many deep and conflicting emotions. Even when a death is expected it takes something special to enable acceptance.

How were we to deal with the death of our son? It was a moment that was hardly expected and, at the time, even further from any chance of being accepted A grandparent, a parent . . . that's different; there are memories to maintain a sense of comfort and consolation. But a child? With the death of a child, even as there are very precious moments that will never be forgotten, the only memories that we had were of the broken dreams and, now, unanswered prayers.

How were we to deal with the death of our son? The answer came the day he was buried, but took a little time for me to understand. The answer came through the lesson of the missing handle.

Do you remember stories about the birth or early days of a loved one who has died?

Did those days have any impact how they lived their life?

Can you tell the story of how they died?

Does that story at all reflect how they lived their life?

How do those stories impact your mourning? Your memories of them? The way you are living your life?

Chapter One

THE FUNERAL WAS PRIVATE. Debby's sisters and many from their families, our son Alex, his girlfriend (Carly, who is now his wife), and one of his closest friends, Alex's rabbi from Scottsdale, and a few others. Our cantorial soloist and the rabbi from the day school that Ricky had attended conducted the service.

I do not know how many funerals I have conducted over the years. 1,500 would not be too far off. Each is unique. Each has its own moment.

The rabbi spoke about Ricky as he knew him and tried to console us by emphasizing that Ricky had a special mission in the world and that we were chosen as his parents because God knew that we could enable him to complete his mission. He spoke of Ricky's kindness and his strength (figuratively and literally—he was a powerlifter), encouraging us to remember him for what he had accomplished and the many he had touched.

Our cantorial soloist read a letter that I had written to Ricky (see below). I had written letters to both of our children at their births and when they celebrated becoming a Bar Mitzvah. I had presented each with their birth letter and had planned on giving them their Bar Mitzvah letters if/when they married, or at some other later, appropriate time. After our cantorial soloist finished reading my letter, I placed the letter I wrote for his becoming a Bar Mitzvah, unopened, on top of the casket. The attendants went to lower the casket, something was wrong. The handle to the lowering device was missing.

It was unique. It was "the moment."

The staff of the cemetery were visibly upset. They were especially sensitive to what was going on because of the many funerals I had conducted and the relationship that we had developed over the years. We, the family, looked at each other, and wondered, out loud, all at the same time: "Ricky?"

It was fitting . . . how were we supposed to handle his death? How were we supposed to find meaning when there was none.

Had he taken it? If he could have, he would have.

A handle was brought from the office and the casket was lowered. Our journey through the valley of the shadow of death began. It is a journey that we are still on. But it is a journey that has begun to offer us the means to handle our loss and our grief. It is a journey that has taught us that the handle had always been there, we were just unable to see it.

I wrote the following letter to Ricky at the time of his birth. Though we thought it had been lost soon after we gave it to him when he celebrated becoming a Bar Mitzvah, we found it neatly folded on a shelf in his closet . . . protected and preserved.

8/17/89

Dear Ricky,

This letter is being written later than hoped for, but a bit sooner than expected. Undoubtedly you will have heard the story of your "premature" birth in Rochester . . . our commuting to/from/between Raleigh, Rochester and Buffalo . . . the visits/feedings at the hospital . . . your Bris (which was this afternoon) . . . a countless number of times. The circumstances ended up being the "best of the worst" . . . and in the end the only thing that matters is that you are well.

Your name "Richard Harry" was derived from the names of mother's grandfathers: Richard for Reuben Levy and Harry for Harry Horwitz. Your mother and I met long after both had died so I cannot tell you too much about either of them. The stories I have heard lead me to believe that they were both honest, hardworking men . . . warm Jews . . . and their names are remembered for good. I am proud, therefore, that their legacy lives on . . . as I am sure they would have been proud of you.

I must say, however, that if it is possible to say "as the children so the parents" . . . then a better name could not be found. Your grandparents (Mom's parents—Harvey and Esther Levy) are two very special people. Their caring, concern . . . the love they express in everything they do . . . it must have come from somewhere. Their parents taught them well and I hope/pray that who/what they are—the legacy passed down to them—is reflected in the name we have chosen for you. To be like them would be an accomplishment that would prove you worthy of their "name" . . . an accomplishment the likes of which could not be "bettered" (I know my grammar needs some work, but I hope you understand what I mean).

For several weeks now I have wondered why you rushed to enter this world. What was it that you expected? Why couldn't you wait? Don't get me wrong . . . we are thankful—consider ourselves lucky/blessed—that you arrived safe and sound. But 8 weeks early and 3.3 lbs. is hardly what one would consider "full-term". Though the answer to that question will never be known, I hope, in retrospect that you will have found good reason for everything that has happened in your life this far.

When I hold you in my arms and watch you begin to discover just what kind of world this is I marvel at the miracle of birth—of life itself.

Do you know how much we love and cherish the opportunity we have been granted to guide you and teach you?

Do you know how much we love and cherish the opportunity we have been granted to learn from you . . . rediscover the wonder life holds for us?

Do you know how much we love and cherish you?

Sitting here—in your grandparents' house—I think about what the next years will bring. Will we provide for you . . . will we respond to you . . . will we be there for you? I want nothing more from life than to be able to answer "Yes" to those questions . . . but right now I can only pledge that we will do our best.

My dream for you is that as you grow you learn to appreciate what really is important in life . . . that you do find life meaningful and significant. I want you to be whatever it is that you want to be . . . with the only condition that you do your best at whatever that might be.

There is so much more that I could say . . . but only one more thing needs to be said . . . Ricky, you are a Jew. On this day that we welcomed you into the covenant, that you are a Jew seems to be the most important part of your existence. Your history and heritage (your part/role in that history) reaches back much farther than July 6, 1989 . . . it extends all the way back to the beginning of creation. As those of every other generation you will encounter the good and the bad . . . the righteous and the wicked. . . . There is no magic formula for how to make sense out of this world, but the closest we can come is through what our faith teaches us to do. I hope and pray that you find the wisdom to see that though life is not always what we want it to be . . . it is only as a Jew (living a Jewish life) that life will become everything it can be

I will end my "sermon" and hope that one day, as you read these words, you will know that what I am trying to say is that even as I have told you how much I love you, so do I pray that you will accept my efforts . . . know that I have tried my best.

- Believe Ricky—believe in yourself . . . believe in Gd . . . believe that life is worth living.
- Forgive me my mistakes—they were filled with good intentions.
- Hear what I wanted to say even when I was silent.
- Know that we want nothing more for you than what you want for yourself.

You rushed to get here. . . . I will do my best to make that "rush" worth it . . . and for everything I may or may not give you, understand that what you have given to us is more than anyone could have hoped for out of life.

My hopes, my dreams, my prayers, my love are for you . . .

Your father

8/17/89 . . . 16–17 Av 5749

What would you have liked to tell the person you mourn when they were alive?

What did you do with them and for them that gave expression to how you felt about them?

What are you most proud of regarding your relationship with them?

What was missing from your relationship that might have made it even more meaningful and significant?

What do you need to get a handle on your grief? Where would you find that handle?

Chapter Two

I DO NOT BELIEVE that it is by accident that The Psalmist (Psalm 23) describes the mourning process as a journey through "The Valley of the Shadow of Death." Though the sun shone through the days of our *shiva*, there seemed to be only darkness all around.

I have witnessed the *shiva* period turned into everything but what it is supposed to be:

- The word itself is used as a verb.

- The period has become transformed into anywhere from the afternoon after the funeral to three days.

- Any talk about the deceased is discouraged . . . it is too sad.

So, what is *shiva*? The word *shiva* is Hebrew for the number seven and it refers to the initial period of mourning after the funeral when mourners are to refrain from engaging in the world of everyday affairs and focus, instead, on the one who has died.

It is a difficult period. Sometimes it seems as if it will last forever. Sometimes it feels like it ended before it began. Sometimes I think it refers to the number of pounds you gain eating all of the comfort food that seems to be everywhere rather than the number days that one "sits." However, it can also bring a great deal of comfort and consolation . . . even satisfaction (which, if one wants to play with the Hebrew letters making up the word *shiva*, could be said to be an alternative translation). How so? Consider the "Valley."

Why is the mourning process compared to a valley? Because, like a valley, there is an entrance and an exit; a beginning and an end. Yes, the mourning process is meant to force us to embrace the darkness and grief that envelope us. However, we are only allowed to dwell within its shadow for so long. At the end of *shiva* one must get up, go out, and get going again.

Why is the mourning process compared to a valley? Because, like a valley, it is open to all. When we grieve, we are not alone. Some may share our sadness. Some may (re)focus on their own. However, as we walk from one end to the other, we are accompanied by others.

And yet, as apt as the image might be, it also poses a few challenges.

First, as we walk through that valley, others who accompany us may walk at a different pace. Some will go slower, not wanting to exit when the time arrives. Some may run as fast as they can, finding the darkness too scary. Some will try to avoid it all together, walk around, or climb any mountain they can to avoid that part of the journey. Those "somes" will do what they think they need to do.

For the mourner? It is during *shiva* that you find out who your real friends are. There are some who I thought would be there to listen, even if that meant hearing the same thing over and over again as I tried to process the moment. There were some who I thought would do the polite visitation because they thought they had to. I had only one expectation that week . . . that was to have none . . . to try to stay in touch with what I was really thinking and feeling. That was a good thing. For the most part, if I had had any expectations of how others might respond to our grief, I would have been overwhelmingly disappointed and surprised. Those I thought I could count on did everything they could to avoid any substantive conversation. The ones who I thought were being polite often had the greatest presence. People tried their best, but many were afraid of the contagion. . . . They were afraid that if they got too close, the same might happen to them. I cannot count how many people took out their cell phones and called their own children even before they left from visiting us.

Intellectually, I knew all of that. I have spent a good part of my career counseling grieving families. However, I also knew that if I were to be overly intellectual, I would not give Ricky the tribute he deserved . . . not the least of which meant creating a response to his death that would preserve his legacy. So, rather than having open visitation at our home, we invited those who wished to comfort us join us at the synagogue for our *minyan* (daily service held in the morning and the afternoon). I felt that the place would help determine the nature of the moment and keep it focused on what it was supposed to accomplish. In some ways it did.

That first afternoon we had to move the service into the sanctuary; the chapel was too small. That there were so many who cared was comforting. And yet, as I looked around, I saw too much pain on their faces. Their angst was making things worse, not better. At one point I walked up on the *bimah* (raised stage like platform from which we conducted our services), picked up a portable microphone and began to talk . . . unrehearsed and without any prior intent. I told two stories.

First, a story about grief. When we mourn, we have the obligation of saying *Kaddish*. It is a strange prayer that does not mention death. In fact, it is really a doxology, a praise of God. Why would we pause to praise God when, in the midst of our grief, there are other words that come to mind in much stronger terms? As the story is told, when a person dies, God looks down at creation and weeps. As counterintuitive as it sounds, because of the loss, God finds His creation diminished . . . the world has gotten smaller. God weeps? God feels the loss? We immediately reach out to praise God in order to offer our comfort and consolation. Strange? Perhaps. But it teaches an important lesson. When we weep, there is One who weeps with us. When we mourn, there is One who mourns with us. When we are searching for meaning, there is One who is at our side wanting to help us along our way.

Second, a story about death. We are taught that after death, whenever that person's name is mentioned, their lips move from within the grave. It is as if they are still among us, a part of us, even as they seem so far apart from us. The story teaches us that the conversation can continue.

To make those stories my own, at each service I found a moment to teach three passages from a different chapter of *Pirke Avot* (a treatise of ethical sayings of our sages). That pause enabled us to say an additional *Kaddish* and gave me an opportunity to mention Ricky's name, even if I was the only one who heard me say it.

That Tuesday night, Hebrew High (which meets in our building) suspended classes and came down to participate in the *minyan*. The teachers looked pale. I could only imagine them thinking about their own children who were, for the most part, babies. The students looked scared. They did not know what to expect. From the looks on their faces, they seemed concerned regarding how *their* rabbi was dealing with the death of his son. I had been there for many of them for *simchas* (happy occasions) and sorrows, but I am not sure that they ever considered me a regular human being until that evening. I skipped the text I was going to speak about and talked about making a *shiva* call. I acknowledged the raging and conflicting emotions that accompany such a visit: not knowing what to expect, being a little concerned about our own families . . . feeling vulnerable. I also talked about that moment as a *mitzvah*.

A story: A young boy was given the task of moving a large boulder from the middle of a field. He pushed at it, pulled at it, shouted at it, cursed it, spoke nicely to it, did everything he could think of, but it just would not move. Over the course of his struggle a large crowd had gathered on the edge of the field bombarding him with all sorts of unsolicited advice. The more they yelled, the more distressed the young boy became. Finally, an older man walked up to the young boy and asked him what he was trying to do. The boy explained that he was trying to move the rock, and that he had tried absolutely everything to no avail. The older man put his arm around the young boy's shoulder and told him that there was one thing he had not yet done. He had not asked for help. With that the two of them joined together and the rock rolled out of the way. That, I told the students, is what a *shiva* call is all about.

It is a cosmic hug that enables us to roll the boulders blocking our way out of the way.

Some of the comments we heard from our friends were beyond belief:

- After telling me how sorry they were for our loss, one couple then went on for 10 minutes about how they had had trouble with their children, too. Fortunately, they told me, they were OK.

- After telling us how sorry he was for our loss, another friend told us that he was sick over his daughter's marriage . . . how the worst thing a parent could ever do is watch their child go through a divorce. We wanted to ask him how that measured up against watching a coffin get lowered into the ground.

- "What can I do for you?" I was asked so many times. "Get me a time machine" was my only response, which caused not a few to turn on their heels and walk away.

And then there were those who had lost children or siblings themselves. They would just look me in the eye and share a tear. "You know," I would say in response. And that meant more than anything anyone else said or did.

I will forever say Ricky's name. Our conversation will go on. As to the *Kaddish*? I said it as faithfully as I could, not just for the required 30 days, but for 11 months (he had no one else to say it for him). "Don't cry," I was told at his birth. At his death there were times that I felt God's tears.

In the midst of mourning, what is the worst or best thing anyone said to you?

What would you have liked people to have said?

Why is shiva so important? What happens when we do not take the time to acknowledge the loss?

What is the difference between a celebration of life and actually mourning the death of a loved one?

- *Which is easier?*

- *Which is more important for our well-being?*

How will your experience of grief and mourning impact the way that you will engage with your friends and family when they have a death?

When The Psalmist speaks about traveling through a valley, he also tells us that goodness and mercy are pursuing us . . . not just following us, pursuing us . . . so that we might be able to dwell in the House of the Lord—find peace.

- *What have you learned about yourself and the way you value life from the mourning experience?*

- *What are the goodness and mercy that are pursuing you?*

- *From where have you found your sense of peace and/or consolation?*

What do you need to get a handle on your grief? Where would you find that handle?

Chapter Three

AT FIRST, SITTING *SHIVA* left me feeling very vulnerable. Those prayers. What did they mean to me now? How am I expected to praise God or to find meaning in a world that seemed to have none?

Prayer had always been important to me. Even though there were times when the reading seemed rote, still, I always came away with something. In the wake of Ricky's death all I saw were black smudges on a clean white page.

And yet, even as the questions were many, I also remembered an incident from my student pulpit in Blountville, TN. I visited there as a student rabbi twice a month and during the High Holy-days for three years. In retrospect, they taught me more than I ever gave to them. Especially when it came to prayer.

The main service at that congregation was the late Friday night Shabbat service. We used the old Silverman prayer book (the hallmark of the Conservative movement at that time). Wanting to make the service ever more meaningful, I tried to augment the form of our worship in a number of different ways. One night, I decided to try something very different. After the recitation of the *Amidah* (the core of the service), which is silent, I asked that we pause for a moment of silent prayer—"having recited the words that mean so much, let us add our own words from the bottom of our hearts." Everyone dutifully bowed their heads, and, after a moment, I led the congregation in *Oseh Shalom* (a prayer for peace). No one walked out so I thought that the moment had been well received.

Then came the *oneg* (a reception held after the service). I noticed a group of lay leaders standing in a corner, talking and glancing furtively in my direction. I knew something was up. Their designated spokesman approached me and said, "Rabbi, we know that you are trying to make our services more meaningful, and we appreciate everything that you are doing. However, what you did tonight was very distracting. I cannot tell you how hard it is for us to stop and begin to pray in the middle of a service." I am not sure if I choked on my tea before he realized what he had said. I just smiled. He mentioned something about having to rethink what he just said, and what I had done. From that week on, the moment of silent prayer became a moment that was embraced with great anticipation.

Jews *daven* (dutifully recite the proscribed liturgy), we do not "pray." If that had been an evangelical church and I asked someone to pray the words would have emerged without any hesitation . . . meaningfully and meaningful. However, ask a Jew to pray and the tongue cleaves to the roof of the mouth. We can say any number of blessings (*b'rachot*), but prayers? The conversation at that Friday evening service from so many years ago echoed loudly in my ears. How could I pray in the midst of the service? What was the purpose of my prayer?

I have been taught a number of reasons for prayer. I have been taught that there is a theurgical element to prayer, that it affects "On High." I have been taught that there is a humanistic element to prayer, that it has nothing to do with God, and everything to do with me. I do not believe that God is vending machine, that I am supposed to put the right prayer in and receive a candy bar (an answer to my prayer) in return. And in the midst of *shiva*, even as I knew of all of those elements, I found it extremely hard to stop and begin to pray in the middle of the service. Until . . .

The Shabbat during *shiva* I went to one of the local Orthodox congregations. Though I would not take an *aliyah* (be called up to say the blessings over the reading of a section from the weekly Torah portion), when the time came for the *Hatzi Kaddish* (a piece very similar to the Mourner's *Kaddish*) during the Torah service, the rabbi called me up. Even as my legs froze, I wanted to run as fast as I could. Somehow, I approached the *bimah* and, after a moment that seemed like an eternity, I chanted that *Kaddish*. As the words came out, I remembered that evening in Tennessee, and I remembered that story about the purpose of saying *Kaddish* is to praise God. Somewhere there was The One who was crying with me, who felt the same pain that I did. And I realized, the purpose of prayer is not for me to talk to God, the purpose of prayer is for me to listen to God speaking to me.

Where is that voice heard? The foundation of Jewish prayer (the base that it is modeled on) is the sacrificial cult. God calls out to the people to bring sacrifices (*korbanot*) at very specific times for very specific reasons. The root of the work *korban* means to draw near. We bring the sacrifice, God draws near, we are embraced by God's presence. We don't ask for anything. We do not put a nickel in a machine and hope for a candy bar to come out. We draw near to God to seek a glimmer of God's presence, a sense of God's closeness.

I needed to change my focus and listen to what God was trying to tell me. By the end of *sheloshim* (the first 30 days of mourning), which fell on the day before Rosh HaShannah, I began to hear it. On Yom Kippur, after *Yizkor* (the memorial service), I shared the following with the congregation. How I said it I still do not know. But the reason and the need were too important for me not to say it:

> For the past 18 years that we have been together I do not think that I have asked much of you from a personal perspective. This year, however, I want to ask for a moment . . . and your understanding that it might take me a moment to say what I need to share with you.
>
> When our son Ricky died this past summer, as I am sure you understand—we are no different from any other people—our world fell apart. There were no words . . . nothing seemed to make sense. And, in order to begin to put Humpty Dumpty back together, we began the work of mourning.

For those who have been there . . . and we all are mourners more often than we want to remember . . . while sitting *shiva*, and then trying to endure the "new normal" . . . our emotions bounce around like a ping pong ball in a shoebox. I, for one, become hyper vigilant and hypersensitive . . . and this time that vigilance and sensitivity revolved around the liturgy—what has given me so much strength and comfort over the years raised many more questions than I could have imagined.

And yet . . .

One morning during shiva I noticed something I had never thought about before—it was in the preliminary service, when we read "The Song of The Sea," the grammar of which has inspired volumes of commentary. It says (Exodus 15):

$$אָ֣ז יָשִֽׁיר־מֹשֶׁה֩ וּבְנֵ֨י יִשְׂרָאֵ֜ל$$
$$אֶת־הַשִּׁירָ֤ה הַזֹּאת֙ לַֽיהֹוָ֔ה וַיֹּאמְר֖וּ לֵאמֹ֑ר$$

lit: אָ֣ז "Then" (past tense) יָשִֽׁיר "will sing" (future).

How can that be? There are all sorts of explanations that make more or less sense. That one day, however, instead of struggling with the grammar, I let go and read the liturgy for what it is. Interestingly, I noticed the verses that precede the song itself . . . the verses that include this note:

$$וַיַּֽאֲמִ֙ינוּ֙ בַּֽיהֹוָ֔ה וּבְמֹשֶׁ֖ה עַבְדּֽוֹ$$

"that the people believed in God and in Moses"—which is then immediately followed by: אָ֣ז יָשִֽׁיר־מֹשֶׁה֩—then he sang that song.

I am not Moses—never thought of myself as such, never want to be. And yet, those verses spoke to me as never before. What were they trying to say? They were saying that because of the support, the strength, the comfort and compassion of his community, Moses was able to take the steps that would lead them closer to the Promised Land . . . he was able to sing his song . . . he was able to move forward.

I am not Moses—never thought of myself as such, never want to be. However, the text made me realize that

I had experienced (was in the midst of) a "Moses Moment" myself. How was I supposed to take the steps that would lead me closer to the Promised Land . . . be able to sing a song . . . be able to move forward. I could not do it alone . . . but because of what you extended to us I saw not only that I could, but that I would.

What am I trying to say? What is this moment I am taking all about? Essentially it is that I want to thank you from the bottom of my heart for the support, the strength, the comfort and compassion that you have extended to us . . . the cards, the tributes, the stories, the meals, the efforts you made to ensure that we had a minyan so we could say *Kaddish* for the required 30 days . . . none of that (and none of you) went unnoticed or unappreciated.

So, for this moment that I have taken . . . to the staff who did more than I know (but I have my sources and am finding out), to each of you who reached out to us and for us as you did . . . I want to say thank you . . . for your efforts, for your time, for being the people that you are—the community that we can pride ourselves in being, there are not enough words, but there is our eternal appreciation.

Thank you . . . and may you (we all) have a year where the only moments we will share are filled with *health*, happiness and peace.

That "thank you" was a reflection of my prayer. In it I tried to capture the voice of God that I had begun to hear.

How important to you is prayer?

Has your grief or mourning impacted your desire and/or capacity to pray?

Take a minute and compose a prayer of your own.

- *How hard was it to write your prayer?*
- *How is it the same as or different from what we are used to finding in our prayerbook?*
- *How important is this prayer to you?*

Does prayer always have to be to/for/about God?

How can prayer help you get a handle on your grief?

Can prayer help you get a handle on your grief?

Chapter Four

AFTER RICKY DIED, DEBBY and I found ourselves spending much more time together. We were not doing anything different than what we normally had . . . just more of it. The one difference was that, for the most part, the time that we spent in the car was focused on Ricky: our memories, our sense of loss, our mourning. Some of the conversations were painful, some were helpful. One that I remember best was when, in the midst of a tense conversation Debby asked quite bluntly: "Do you believe in God?" Fortunately, I had to get my eyes back on the road, swerve to avoid an accident, and was able to change the whole course of our conversation to a very different topic.

"Do you believe in God?" When congregants come to me with questions regarding their belief, often saying that they do not believe in God, I usually respond very quickly with: "Oh really? Which one?" I do not answer in that manner to be flippant, but to make a point about faith.

When tending to a few legal matters at a bank the woman I was working with was visibly shaken by our story of Ricky's death. She looked at me and, with tears in her eyes, said: "My brother just lost his wife. I know it is not exactly the same. However, I envy you your faith. It is what got him through his sorrow, and I am sure it will help you as well." She knew I was a rabbi, but at that moment I wondered if I was. What did I believe?

I firmly believe that doubt is the first step toward faith. We need to continually question if we are to remain engaged with what we actually do believe. The questioning enables us to transform thought into practice. After all, our values are not what we say we believe, but are reflected in what we actually do. And what I do is determined by the type of God in which I believe, especially if that God is the one I see in the mirror or the one I find to be that much greater than myself.

What do I believe? The options are many. They include:

- I can believe that God is an aged sage, sitting in a throne with staff in hand, directing His heavenly host to do his bidding.

- I can believe that God is like a watchmaker who, after putting all the gears in place and winding it up, leaves it to run on its own.

- I can believe that God is like that Disney character, Jiminy Cricket, sitting on my shoulder counseling me regarding right and wrong.

- I can believe that God is that still small voice within, sort of like my conscience, enabling me to discern between right and wrong.

- I can believe that God is the sum of my experiences, learned and taught, that prevent me from touching a hot stove more than once.

- I can believe that God is all of those things, or none of those things, all at the same time.

Since Ricky died, I have struggled with what I believe. There are times when I have questioned if there is any sort of God at all, any sort of power or force outside of us other than our imagination. There are times when I have firmly believed that God has directed every second of every day and that it is not mine to question anything other than what I am supposed to learn from all of this. And there have been times when I am just numb, so distant from any sort of concern about belief, and just trying to make it through that particular moment (forget about the whole day).

And yet, too many things have made me question my doubt and my faith. Too many moments have emerged that have grabbed me by the shoulders and shaken me to my very core.

There were the moments surrounding the nature and timing of his death: the ICU, the machines, that he died close to his original due date, that he died at the age of 28 (which, in Hebrew letters spells out the word for "strength"—he was a powerlifter). Could all of that only be coincidence? The week we held the unveiling and dedication of the marker on his grave, it seemed to happen again: it was scheduled, we discovered, for the *yahrtzeit* of Debby's father; earlier that week, on the day of my father's *yahrtzeit*, I received a call out of the blue from my sister (with whom I had no contact for several years—since the death of our mother) extending her condolences on Ricky's death. And, on his birthday, a colleague, whose emails and blogs I find personally inspirational, published a piece: "Three Lessons I Learned from a Grieving Father."

How can all of that be explained? Was it all coincidence? Was there a sign? . . . a message? Was I hearing God's voice? If so, what was it saying. Too much to believe straight away. Too much to not believe. But what was I to believe? How was I supposed to put all of this together? Where was that missing handle?

In the Book of Exodus, in the midst of the description of the building of the Tabernacle, Moses confronts God, asking for a face-to-face encounter. Moses is told that no person can see God's face and live. Instead, God suggests that Moses hide in a cave, where his vision will be cut off. God promises to pass by, and then allow Moses to see His back. Kind of strange. Why is God so concerned with anyone seeing Him up close and personal, only allowing a glimpse of His presence after He is gone?

Unless . . . unless there is a lesson here. To see God up front and personal might lead to either a feeling of complete vulnerability (being dependent only and always on what God decides to do), or a certain degree of conceit (feeling that we might be able to persuade God to see things our way). Instead, we are bound to seeing what God does, after the fact. It is then up to us to decide how we are going to respond. Will we follow God and God's ways? Or will we just let God go on, while we go off to do whatever we want? Were all of the "coincidences" signs? Were we seeing God walking in front of us?

Something was missing and, besides Ricky, I did not know what that was.

I remembered a story about Rabbi Meir. While he is in the house of study on a Shabbat afternoon his sons die. When he arrives home his wife asks him a question: "If someone had entrusted a precious treasure to you for safe keeping, with the understanding that one day you would have to give it back, would you accept the responsibility?" "Of course," he replies. "And when the owner of the treasure arrived to collect his belongings would you give what was his back cheerfully, appreciative of the time that it was in your possession?" "Of course," he replies. His wife then leads him into the room where his sons had been prepared for burial.

That story was taught in one of the first homiletics courses I took in rabbinic school. It was a tool to have in our pocket for use in creating a eulogy should the need arise. The first funeral I ever did was at my student pulpit. It was for a young man—my age, height and build—who had dropped dead in front of his mother. When I arrived, prepared with all of my newfound rabbinic wisdom (and that story on the tip of my tongue), the mother took one look at me and passed out. I did not use the story at the funeral.

In fact, I have never used that story. As sweet as it sounds, it is also very harsh. I don't see it offering much comfort to anyone except the one who tells it (and it lets those who come to comfort the mourner off the hook).

And yet, after Ricky died, the story began to make sense. He was not even close to being a *Tzadik* (totally righteous person), but he was a very precious gift. Instead of focusing on the missing pieces in my life, if I were to embrace the gift that he was (and will always be) I would find a bit of God's presence.

Life is not about us. Life is all about us. And God? God has a place in our lives only if and when we are prepared to let Him in. If we are too full of ourselves, thinking that life is only about us, then there is no room for God.

Our sages teach us that strength is measured not in or through the circumference of our biceps but, rather, in the degree to which we control our passions. Ricky died. I wanted to scream "Why? . . . Why me?" And there were moments when I did. However, almost before those questions left the "roof of my mouth" I realized that even as it is all about me, it has nothing to do with me. If God is God, then His greatest strength is the degree to which He controls His passions, gives us free will. If I want to be "Godly" should not I strive to do the same?

An undergraduate professor of mine once said that no one promised us life would be meaningful, but we are guaranteed that it will present us with the opportunity to make meaning. Maybe Ricky was that opportunity. Maybe in so far as that opportunity teaches me to see the world as it really is, I will see God's back/presence as well.

It is as if God wants us to see Him, is waiting for us to open our eyes and our hearts . . . wondering why we will not accept His embrace.

Do you believe in God?

- *Why?*
- *Why not?*

How has your belief in God changed over the course of your lifetime?

What experiences have had an impact on your belief?

Is there a difference between faith and belief?

Which is more important?

How has your mourning had an impact on your faith/belief in God?

Has your mourning had an impact on your faith or belief in God?

How has your faith/belief in God had an impact on your grief or mourning?

Has your faith or belief in God had an impact on your grief or mourning?

How has your faith or belief given you a handle on your grief or mourning?

Chapter Five

I OPENED THE EMAIL from a local colleague, knowing what to expect. Another *simcha*. What a fortunate family. Oh, I am sure they have their own measure of *tzuris* (sorrows), but it seems that every time I turn around they have something to celebrate. Me? I was not quite sure.

Shortly after Ricky died, our oldest son, Alex, became engaged. He and Carly had been together for almost five years, so, in some ways, it did not come as a surprise. In fact, one day during *shiva*, when Alex and I had to go out to take care of a legal matter, in the middle of nowhere he blurted out, "Well, I guess this makes Alex Palmer the best man." Alex is Alex's best friend since childhood. In fact, Alex, who had moved to Phoenix, was in the hospital with us almost the whole time. When we announced the engagement that Shabbat (we have a moment in our service when we pause and ask people to share their *simchas*) there was spontaneous applause. The word spread almost as fast as Ricky's death. People could not wait to wish us *mazal tov*. I could see the relief on their faces . . . now they would not have to watch us mourn. All would be well. Would it? We felt only joy for Alex, but the sorrow had not diminished in the least; in some ways it was exacerbated by the knowledge that Ricky would not be with us.

And yet . . .

Shortly after Pesach I received that email. We were invited to an engagement party at their *shul*. I went. It was a bit surreal.

I looked at the couple, I looked at their families, and wondered whether we looked the same. I wondered whether the joy would ever be set free.

In the midst of the party, one of our preschool teachers came up to me and said that she had to tell me something. It was a bit out of place, but she needed to say it none the less. Since Ricky's death, in response to that moment, she had been making it a point to teach her four-year-old class the *Modeh Ani*—a prayer that is said on arising, giving thanks for the day and all that life will bring us. She told me that she began every class with that prayer as a tribute to the gift that Ricky had been to all of us. I do not remember much more than thanking her; my head sort of began to spin. I was not sure whether to scream, cry, or hug her as tightly as I could.

However, that moment caused me to do something I had put off. We had donated a *yad* (a silver pointer shaped like a *yad*—hand) for reading the Torah to that synagogue as a tribute to Ricky. There was no mention of the donation, no plaque or engraving . . . we just did it. I had not yet seen the *yad*. I asked one of the rabbis if the Ark was accessible. He knew what I wanted. He told me which Torah it was on without even being asked. There was no one in the sanctuary when I went in. I opened the Ark, and when I reached out to touch the *yad*, I felt that it had, instead, touched me.

The missing handle? The missing handle was how long it took me to realize just how much of a gift Ricky was, and will always be. He was far from a *tzadik*. In fact, a whole book could be written on his "who, what, when, where, how, and why." However, he was our Ricky, and the lessons he taught us . . . especially the things that time has reminded us of that we do not remember ever forgetting . . . are timeless.

The missing handle? The missing handle was the realization that even as important as it is to remember, it is that much more important to live so that the memories live on as well.

Consider: In the Book of Numbers, where the wanderings of our ancestors are listed, encampment after encampment for the 40 years they were in the wilderness, we are taught (33:2):

וַיִּכְתֹּב מֹשֶׁה אֶת־מוֹצָאֵיהֶם לְמַסְעֵיהֶם עַל־פִּי יְהוָה וְאֵלֶּה מַסְעֵיהֶם
לְמוֹצָאֵיהֶם:

"Moses recorded (actually wrote down) their departures
according to their journeys by the commandment of the
Lord; and these are their journeys according to their
departures:"

Though it is much more apparent in the Hebrew, in first half
of the verse "their departures" is mentioned before any reference to
the journeys, while in the second half, "their departures" is mentioned last. Different ways of looking at things. One can always
look back, stressing the place from which one has come, yearning
to return to what was. Another way is to look forward, focusing on
our mission, vision, and values . . . yes, standing on the foundation
of what was, but always focused on moving forward. Not easy, but
it enables us to find the handle that we need to make sense out of
that which does not seem to have any.

Shortly before the High Holydays, I received a call from the
editor of the local Jewish newspaper. She needed a rabbi's message
for the High Holydays. She had a deadline approaching and the
rabbi who had been assigned the article was unable to provide it.
She asked if I could forward something that I might be able to dig
up. I went to my files and in the midst of copying a piece from several years ago, I began typing instead. This is what I wrote, which
appeared in the September 22, 2017 issue of *The Arizona Jewish
Post*:

> This past August, while sitting *shiva* for our son Ricky,
> the liturgy at our daily *minyan* took on new and impor-
> tant meaning for me. Passages that were once a source of
> comfort and strength became burdensome and caused
> me to ask more questions than I knew I could answer.
> Other passages, prayers that were meaningful but "rou-
> tine," took on greater significance than I thought pos-
> sible. An example of the latter (a prayer that moved me
> in ways that it never had before) is the short phrase that
> we chant when returning the Torah to the *aron kodesh*

(Ark): *Hadesh yameinu k'kedem*—Renew our days as in the past.

More than anything, that is what I wanted (and, in more ways than one, still do)! If only we could turn back the clock and know what was about to happen: prevent death from occurring. If only . . . if only . . . if only . . . Renew our days as in the past. And yet, as passionately as those words emerged from my heart, so did I also understand that what I wanted would/could not be.

And yet? And yet, those words came to mean even more over the course of our *sheloshim* (the 30-day mourning period for the loss of a child). As the days marched on, that phrase empowered me to understand that more important than looking back over the past was looking forward to the future. More important than getting stuck in the grief was the need to look toward the strength that the memories will provide me . . . the joy that yet can be . . . the opportunity to continue to try to transform this world into what it still can be . . . to make sure that I try to touch the world as Ricky did.

As it was this past August . . . as it has been over the past few weeks . . . so is it even more so as we begin this New Year of 5778. *Hadesh yameinu k'kedem*—Renew our days as in the past. What is it we really want for the New Year? Is it to go back in time and have what was? Or is it to embrace what is ours to have and make the most of it . . . try our best to make the best use of the opportunities that are presented to us day in and day out to move forward into our future?

As we sit on the cusp of the beginning of a New Year, we can look back with desire at what used to be, want to cling to the past and never let go. But then we will only be stuck to what was. What my experience with this prayer taught me is that there is nothing to be had with getting stuck in the past. However, if we strive to build a future based on what made the past (the foundation upon which we stand today) so meaningful and significant, then our days will be renewed with hopes and prayers fulfilled, smiles and laughter for all to share.

And so, as we sit on the cusp of the beginning of a New Year, I share with you what this short phrase has come to mean to me . . . I share my prayer for you:

Hadesh yameinu k'kedem—Renew our days as in the past. Remind us that the present is a gift that we should not take for granted.

Hadesh yameinu k'kedem—Renew our days as in the past. Empower us to transform the opportunities that are afforded us into the reality of a world that is deserving of praise.

Hadesh yameinu k'kedem—Renew our days as in the past. Teach us to appreciate those moments that are ours.

Hadesh yameinu k'kedem—Renew our days as in the past. Enable us to find a little piece of peace.

Hadesh yameinu k'kedem—Renew our days as in the past. May all the goodness that has been ours echo into the days and weeks to come so that we will know what it is to have a *Shannah Tovah* . . . a year of health, a year of happiness, a year of peace.

In the face of the death of a loved one, our first reaction is to focus on our loss. We can only see what is missing. However, when we begin to look around a bit, and focus on what will always be, especially the lessons that we were taught by the presence of those we so loved, something important happens . . . we can begin to understand that even where or when we are not in control, still we are a factor in the equation. Nothing will equal having our loved ones at our side, but the significance they added to our lives need not be lost. In fact, it can become "even more so."

There are some who say that the experience of losing a loved one, especially when "tragic," can send you back to the world with more compassion and understanding. My experience is that I see the world in much sharper shades of black and white. But, I am beginning to see it.

Is there any real compensation for your loss?

Does something good that happens immediately relieve you of your grief?

What can or do people do that makes you "feel better?"

What are you doing that makes you "feel better?"

What are the most important memories of your loved one that you want to preserve?

Understanding that there is no time machine to take you back in time, what would you most pray for in order to Hadesh Yameinu K'kedem?

How has your loss given you a handle on living life to the fullest?

Chapter Six

THERE IS A PHRASE in the Talmud that is the core of every sermon I have ever given: *Ma'ee nafka m'nah*. It appears after opposing viewpoints on a particular topic are presented and is usually understood as: "What is the practical difference?" I have always understood it to mean: "So what? Who cares? What am I supposed to learn (take home) from all of this?" In the Talmud it helps resolve an "argumentative impasse." When used as the core of a sermon it enables me to stay focused on the point of the matter under discussion in the first place. In truth, not much of a difference.

Nu, so, it should be asked: "*Ma'ee nafka m'nah*?" What is this all about? What is the point of this search for the missing handle?

There was a previous moment in my life when I thought that the bottom had fallen out. I had been serving a congregation for nine years and thought that I would be there forever. I liked the people, I liked the weather, and our family was thriving. And then it happened! It was my 10th year. I like to describe the moment as being similar to the story of our ancestors in Egypt: "A new pharaoh arose who knew not Joseph." There was an attempt to change the culture of the congregation. It was awful. All our hopes and dreams and prayers were shattered. I was left contemplating just how to go forward. Was it time to leave the rabbinate? Should I just look for a different congregation? I was told that it was a fight that I would win. However, I was concerned about the people who I had come to know and to love. I decided that for everyone's sake it would be best to resign.

Shortly after my resignation was official, I took a day and went home to see my family. As always, I went to the cemetery and visited loved ones. I remember vividly, after reciting the appropriate prayers, leaning against the headstone and asking out loud, hoping one of them would hear me and give me the answers they always did: "OK, so what am I supposed to be learning from all of this?" I did not hear the voices that I was hoping for, but in the depth of the silence I got the answer that I needed to take my next step forward. The answer was the question itself.

I had to catch my breath. For so long I had been focused on "Why me?" that I had lost sight of the bigger picture. Yes, life had turned very painful. Everything was falling apart. For a while the only thing I could think about was "me" and why my world seemed to be coming to an end. However, when I stepped back and looked at things from a different perspective, I saw that there was an opportunity to move on and move forward. I saw that there was a possibility to live again.

Ricky died. It was déjà vu all over again. And yet, at the same time, there was a practical difference . . . there was a framework within which to move forward . . . there was the search for the missing handle.

Traditionally, from the time of a death until the burial itself, those who are mourners are said to be in a state of *aninut*, "nothingness." Our purpose is to tend to the needs of the decedent. After the burial, the mourners move to a state of *aveilut*, "mourning" It is a time when we begin to embrace the grief and move forward, make the memories live and give our loved ones the living tribute they so deserve. That is not always an easy transition to make. Too often we get stuck in the "in-between." We know that something is missing, that our world will never be the same. However, we do not take the step forward. We need to lean against the moment and ask ourselves: "OK, so what am I supposed to be learning from all of this?" Instead, we get stuck. When finished tending to their final needs, we neglect addressing our own. Instead, we get stuck. We can only ask ourselves: "Why me?" Why does this hurt so much?

Why has my world fallen apart? We fail to go looking for our missing handle.

Ricky died. Whenever we lose a loved one, whether expected or not (and even when expected, there is a big difference between two words that sound very similar: to expect does not necessarily guarantee that one will accept) our world changes significantly. No, Humpty Dumpty cannot be put back together. When we lose a loved one, we are confronted with a challenge: stay stuck where we are, or embrace the grief and begin to construct our "new normal." Do we dwell in the world of "nothingness" or acknowledge the loss and move on; acknowledge that life has changed in a profound manner and that even as we know we will never get over the loss, we can endeavor to live with it? As we find ourselves all too ready to weep, can we also cry?

In order to take that step that led to my search for the missing handle, I had to first realize the difference between real and unreal expectations. To expect an answer to the question (much less have the right to ask): "Why me?" was unrealistic. However, to ask "OK, so what am I supposed to be learning from all of this?" was, in many ways, what was expected of me if I was to begin to embrace my grief.

- I could not expect anyone to be anything other than what they already were.

- I could only expect me to be myself.

- I had to learn to expect to feel pain, to be numb, to wonder, to be angry, to forget, to ___ and sometimes all at the same time.

- I also had to learn to expect to become engaged in the mourning process . . . begin to search for the missing handle.

The day that I wrote this piece I had to take a break and go to the *mikvah* (ritual bath) for the conversion of an adopted one-year-old child. The little girl had been fostered and then adopted and it was time to make her Jewish so her family would be whole. As we proceeded with a little ceremony after the immersion, I could feel the joy . . . the hopes and dreams and prayers . . . of her new (now) parents come alive. I saw the pure innocence on the child's face. I melted in the presence of her big dark eyes and joyful smile. And inside I was coming unglued. All I could think of was Ricky.

Ricky died. So have many others. That is part of life. How are we supposed to respond to death? Are we to take it personally? Rage against the way of the world, screaming "Why me?" Are we to withdraw into the darkness of the valley and, numb as we might be, let life go on around us? Or . . .

I hid behind the role I was playing at that moment and got in my car to go back to the synagogue. On the way, while passing by a high school, I remembered . . .

For the past several years I have been part of a panel at that local high school, along with a minister and an imam, discussing the particulars of our respective faith traditions. The questions are the same each year, and we, as a panel, seem to have our act pretty much under control. This past fall one of the questions came a little too close. We were asked: "How does your faith tradition impact the way you live your life?" I began to answer that question as I had every other year but had to stop. I almost lost it. I apologized for being so emotional, explained that our younger son had died that past August, and went on to explain that without our faith tradition I am not sure I would have made it. Without the rites and ritual of our mourning practice I would have been stuck in the darkness of the valley. And, that I had to believe. Not to believe would have robbed Ricky of the tribute he deserved, of the recognition of even the smallest part of this world that he made better because of his presence.

The rituals made a difference in my grief and my life. They gave me a framework for processing death and life, and love and loss. They forced me to embrace the past, that then present moment, and the possibility of having a future. And the one ritual which offered me the most was the saying of the Mourners' *Kaddish*, and the community that that act created (or actually, more correctly, exposed).

When I meet with families to discuss a funeral, I describe what I call " the Raytheon Nod." Raytheon is a defense contractor that is one of the largest employers in Tucson. Several congregants work there and, for the most part, the work they do is classified and they cannot talk about it on any level, with anyone, especially each other. I have noticed, however, something I call the Raytheon Nod. It is that nanosecond of recognition when two engineers pass each other. There is a subtle blink of an eye or a nod of the head in which a whole conversation takes place. And, as important as it might be for those engineers, that nod is also indispensable to the process of mourning.

When one first begins to say *Kaddish* the world seems to be dark, we feel all alone. However, as the days pass, we begin to notice that there are others in the room as well. Some are there to say *Kaddish* themselves, some are there because they once found themselves saying *Kaddish* and want to make sure the appropriate quorum is available for others to do the same, some are there to pray, some are there to talk to each other (I like to joke that when I look out at the congregation I often feel that Goldstein came to talk to God, but is having a tough time because everyone else came to talk to Goldstein). And, as we begin to take notice of those "others" their presence offers us a great deal of comfort. "They know." . . . We can tell from the way they look at us. They do not need to say anything; the way they look at us, the expression on their faces says it all. It is that Raytheon Nod. And one day, after a while, someone new enters our world to say *Kaddish*. We see them, we recognize ourselves. We offer them the Nod. We realize how far we have come, how far we still have to go, and that taking/making the journey is the best tribute we can give the ones we so loved.

The rites and rituals, especially when I found them hard to do, were what enabled me to engage in the journey through the "Valley." Perhaps it has to do with what I understand to be neuroplasticity—the ability of the brain to change, to adapt function based on form. Perhaps that is just the way we are wired. Whatever the reason, that is the way I found my world to be.

When those students asked me that question, emotional as my answer might have been, it was a turning point for me (one of many). It was a moment when I realized that more important than mourning my loss was mourning that we had lost him; that his hopes and dreams and prayers would be no more; that if any sense was to be made from any of this it would be through the way we embraced the new normal that was now ours, and make sure that (ritually . . . formally) he would always have a place by our side.

Nu . . . *Ma'ee nafka m'nah* . . . What are we supposed to take away from all of this? At least the understanding that our memories will be for us what we make of them: a burden holding us back or the stuff from which life can continue; always the same, never the same, but worth living because of everything that they were to us and for us . . . everything they will forever be to us and for us.

What differences have you experienced in your life since the death of your loved one?

What differences have you made in your life since the death of your loved one?

What is the greatest attribute, strength or character trait of your loved one that you have tried to make your own?

How has your loss impacted the way that you engage with others who are mourning?

What do you miss the most?

What is keeping you from finding "your handle?

Chapter Seven

A FEW MOMENTS BEFORE discovering that the handle was missing, our cantorial soloist read the letter I had written to Ricky in place of a eulogy. I include it here because, in some ways, it is the handle that I had looked (and continue to look) for. Between the lines the letter reflects that even as the loss is ours, even more importantly, it is and was Ricky's. He had a place in this world, and in our lives, which is irreplaceable. That there was an obstacle to our lowering him into the grave reflects how we, too, needed to pause before letting him go. The descent would happen, the grave would be filled. But those few moments of waiting until the handle arrived proved that he would always be with us. Obviously not the way we would have wished, but here just the same. That is life. That is death. The more we see each particular moment as a part of the greater whole, the more the hole in our heart will begin to heal. Where is meaning to be had when there does not seem to be any? Where we look for it and where we make it; where it always was, and will forever be.

> August 20, 2017
>
> Dear Ricky,
> It is very surreal to be writing this to you right now . . . sitting in the waiting room outside the ICU. However, in the same manner as I wrote you a letter when you were born, which I gave to you when you became a Bar Mitzvah (which I am not sure if you ever read, but I am absolutely positive that you lost) . . . and I wrote to you when you became a Bar Mitzvah, which I was planning to give you at the next major lifecycle moment . . . I think

this moment deserves a few thoughts as well. Though I am not sure if I am writing this to you or for me, in the end, it really does not matter.

I am not sure if it is coincidence, ironic or if there is a message here . . . though it is absolutely confusing and overwhelming . . . there is something about this moment—it is a reflection of how you came into this world: rushing (emerging before your time), sustained by ventilators, IVs, flashing monitors and the chirping of whirring machines. Where you are rushing to this time, or why, I have no idea. However, you always lived your life your way, so I have learned not to question (or at least try).

We were never two of the great communicators. Much of what we shared was in shorthand and in code. I would like to think that what we said to and with each other was shared equally and, that through my very obvious frustration that you did not have the same life experience at your age that I have at mine, you know that I have, and will always, love you.

So why am I writing this to you? Because I want you to know a few of the things that I learned from you:

First, I learned that if you are going to do something, do it "your way" and all the way. When engaged in noble pursuits that formula enabled you to achieve goals no one ever dreamed of: you lost weight, you learned to ride a bicycle when the experts said you never would, you excelled in powerlifting and you were a friend (loyal to the end—even to those who did not deserve it). Unfortunately, you also, sometimes, fell victim to the demons that pursued you and responded in kind to/with them as well.

Second, I learned that when life is challenging, don't back down. And, you certainly had your challenges. You never really seemed to find your perfect niche—though you had many circles of friends. You did not seem to fit into the expectations that life sometimes imposes on us. You appeared to sometimes feel awkward or out of place. I once described you to myself as a Ferdinand the Bull sort of character—in the field, but distracted from the rest of the herd. However, none of that ever stopped you from being you.

Third, I learned that in spite of everything that may or may not happen, skinned knees are just that, skinned knees. Get up and get going again

I am realizing that there is/was much more to you that we did not know about . . . some of which I wish I was still ignorant of. And yet, that was who you are . . . and for someone who was not supposed to even make it past the first few days of your life, you did pretty good for most of your 28 years.

One of the areas in/with which you did your best was as a son, a brother, a nephew and a cousin. Family was first. Though I will always be thankful that mom had unlimited texting . . . that she was so concerned regarding where you were and what you were doing was a reflection of your love to and for each other. You were loyal as a brother, "as one" as a cousin and always conscious of how important it was to be part of an "us."

I look at you now sustained by ventilators, IVs, flashing monitors and the chirping of whirring machines and want to think back to the better years . . . when you would come around the corner from Heim singing and smiling . . . we would ride bikes together—yours with one training wheel, which everyone looked at, but you didn't care . . . listening to you talk with your attorney at all hours of the day . . . and the car(s)—how we thought you were living out of; or could have if you wanted to (tuna on the floor, clothes in the trunk, water in the back seat and who knows what in the glove compartment!) . . . the "Cheese –Its"—a very select club that will never be the same again . . . and your penchant for the latest fashion in towels. Regrets? Only that I was never able to completely understand you and the choices that you made. You accomplished more than anyone thought you would or could (beginning with living life in the first place!) and inspired many by the examples and the mistakes. You saw the world in the deepest shades of black and white . . . especially your politics . . . but your presence illuminated our world in vibrant shades of the colors of the rainbow. What we did not know . . . what you kept secret or chose not to share . . . will always plague us. But the gifts that you shared will never betray us.

There is little that anyone can say that makes even the slightest bit of sense at a time like this . . . no one makes an appointment in life to sit and watch their son die before their eyes. However, where words fail, the hopes and dreams and prayers that can still be yours emerge to take their place. I said the *Vidui* (traditional Jewish confessional that is said at the time of death) with and for you this evening . . . I know religion was not your thing (though you did often dance around the house chanting the Torah service), but the faith that you had in yourself is something that will always be an example for all of us to emulate.

August 22, 2017

You gave us a gift these past few days, allowing us to reflect on you and your story . . . learn how to begin to cope with what will be a missing piece in our hearts and souls. And yet, in return for that gift, so is it ours to give you the same . . . so is it ours to allow you a little piece of peace. In Hebrew, every letter is associated with a number. 28 would spell *ko-ach*—strength. Your strength of body and strength of character are/were not to be taken for granted. And, I hope/pray that whatever might happen over the next few days, you will go from strength to strength. I am not sure how long it will take me to process these past few days. The time I spent sitting by your side reading and praying and questioning and wondering were as moving as they were deeply painful. When we said our final goodbyes and left, I could only think of one thing: as proud as we were that every night you would *come home* (in good times and in bad) . . . finding a safe place to rest and get ready to begin again, so do I hope and pray that as you *go home* you find the same. You will be missed . . . you will be mourned . . . but, most important of all, you will be remembered.

We will always love you . . .

Take a few moments and write a letter to the one whom you mourn.

- *What do you want to tell them?*
- *How much of the letter is about you?*
- *How much of the letter is about them?*

Understanding that death is as much a part of life as life is a part of death, what are some of the things for which you are most thankful regarding your loved one and/or the relationship you had with them?

What do you regret?

Some say that it is better to have had and to have lost than to never have had at all.

- *Do you believe this?*
- *What would your world or life be like if you had never had the relationship that you had with the one you mourn? What are some things they taught you?*

How do you handle loss and disappointment?

What do you do to make yourself feel better?

Chapter Eight

WHEN I WAS IN rabbinic school, I remember being taught that every rabbi has one or two sermons that are theirs. Every rabbi has one book that is theirs.

I know which sermons are mine. I have given them in various forms many times over the years.

My book? The book I fantasized writing is very different from this that I have put together. I do not know if or where it will go from here. Part of me sees these words as the naked rage of a grieving father. Another part wants to share my journey through "The Valley" with the hope that others might find how to better put one step in front of the other . . . a version of my own Raytheon Nod.

I do know one thing for sure: that, with Ricky's first *yahrtzeit* just days away, though I have wept (openly and when alone) innumerable times over the past year, as I place a final period on this page, finally, I can cry.

There was a time when, especially while in a professional role, if I found myself breaking up or needing to cry, I would pause, take a breath, apologize, and then continue with whatever I was doing. Now, however, I do not apologize. One of the most important things I have learned is how crucial it is to stay in touch with how I really feel. Not everyone is happy with that. People get embarrassed or uncomfortable around those who share their emotions out loud. I am not sure why. However, I do know that part of my missing handle is made of tears, so I cry.

I cry with sadness for the broken dreams and promises

I cry with frustration for the opportunities that are no more

I cry with pain and loneliness for the emptiness that envelopes us

I cry with joy for that which we did have

I cry with gratitude for the lessons that he taught us by his very being

I cry with peace, knowing that as long as we remember him, his lips will move . . . he will be a part of us even as he is so far apart from us.

Do you ever find yourself crying?

- *Is there any particular place or activity that triggers your tears?*

- *Do you hide your sadness from others?*

- *Is there anyone in particular with whom you can share your sadness?*

Do you ever find yourself laughing and feeling good about the person who died, and that you had them in your life for as long as you did?

- *Is there any particular place or activity that triggers your joy?*

- *Do you hide your gratitude from others?*

- *Is there anyone in particular with whom you can share how you feel when everything is good?*

After The Afterward

FIVE YEARS HAVE PASSED. And, even though there are times when it feels *k'ilu lo hayah* (as if Ricky, the years spent, his death, and our mourning, never ever were), it also feels as if the moments surrounding his hospitalization, death and burial have yet to end. Much has happened over these years, and they have helped me get a handle on things (sorry for the pun, but hopefully you will see why I say that).

GOING FROM G-O-D TO D-O-G

Shortly after Ricky died, I realized that I had to make certain changes in my life, not the least of which involved how much longer I might want to remain in the pulpit. My contract was up for renewal in the spring of 2020, when I would have served the congregation for 21 years (a major part of the 39 years I served as a full-time pulpit rabbi). I decided that it was time to move on. I informed the congregation in the fall of 2018 that I would not be seeking renewal and began to plan for the future.

Alex, our oldest son, was living in Phoenix, settling into married life and talking about family. Guess where we ended up! We are seven minutes away. Why does any of this matter? Because concurrent with our transition, the world was already moving into the era of COVID-19. And, in the early part of that era, quarantine and lock downs were the norm. Not much to do, no place to go. Alex and Carly were working from home. I walked their dog,

Piper, for them. Now having grown up in a house where you were never supposed to buy anything you had to feed, a dog was a very new experience, but, in some ways, the best thing that could have happened.

If Piper could talk, one of us would have to disappear. For along every one of our routes, there were always those moments when I would ask, "Piper, do you remember Ricky?" She would usually either ignore me (and continue looking for something or someplace to smell) or just pause for a moment and look up at me. Piper was my therapy dog. She listened. And that was what I needed, more than anything else.

Mourning is hard work. Elisabeth Kubler-Ross spoke of five stages of grief: Denial, Anger, Bargaining, Depression, and Acceptance. There were times when people thought of these stages as sequential; even asked mourners where they thought they were (or, even worse, told them what stage they might be in). My own experience, personally and professionally is that these responses to death are not sequential at all. One goes back and forth, or might even feel more than one way at the same time. When mourning, I did not need to be told what stage of grief I was in; neither did I need to categorize my feelings within an academic framework. What I needed was someone to listen. I needed someone who would hear what I had to say and let me say it the way it needed to be said. Piper listened. And the more walks we went on, the more I was able to talk. The more I was able to remember about Ricky's life and our relationship. The more I was able to process his death.

The way our tradition describes a *shiva* call (when one goes to visit and offer comfort to the mourner), one is not to speak until the mourner engages in a comment or initiates a conversation. Our purpose is not to offer unsolicited sage advice, or stories of our own experience (or, as happens more often than not, avoid the subject of death, grief and mourning entirely). Our purpose is to be there to listen. Sometimes there is silence (though more is said in the silence than in any of the conversations).

It took too long, but I realized on one of those walks that I had finally listened to the point of so many sermons I had delivered over the years. Moving to Phoenix and starting life over, this time with family as the center of it all, was the only thing I could have done. It took Ricky's death to teach me to listen to my own heart. It took my grief to teach me to share what I heard with others (or, at least with Piper).

THE LADY IN THE BANK

Earlier, in Chapter 4, I wrote about my encounter with the lady in the bank who told me she was envious of my faith. There is more to that story.

As that woman shared her thoughts with me, my world went blank. It was as if time stopped. All I wanted to do was run to the car and have my "Hollywood moment": bang on the steering wheel and scream at the top of my lungs. However, when I got to the car and sat behind the wheel, it was more like a moment from *A Chorus Line*, when Morales hears about the death of Mr. Karp and feels nothing. That is the way I felt. I felt nothing. But, that I was feeling at all, had broken through the numbness and the rabbinic shell within which I had been hiding, enabled me to move forward.

I had been taught, based on a quote attributed to a sage of the Conservative Movement, Dr. Louis Finkelstein (himself, perhaps, quoting an earlier source), to believe that: "When I pray, I speak to God; when I study, God speaks to me." However, immediately after sitting in the car as I did, I realized that God is not a vending machine: No matter how many coins I put in I would not see a time machine coming down the chute that would enable me to turn back the clock and prevent Ricky's death. No, the only way I would be able to make sense out of anything would be to flip the quote: "When I pray, God speaks to me; when I study, I speak to/ with God." It was time for me to listen (something Piper knew all along). And I found "proof," as it were, in one prayer in particular.

In the second paragraph of the *Amidah* (the central prayer of every service) we read: "You support the falling, heal the sick, free the captive, and keep faith with those who sleep in the dust."

In what I would call traditional "prayer speak" the words are understood as a plea for God to do all of those things, despite this paragraph being in a section of the *Amidah* that is understood as an effort to give praise. It is as if, as we speak to God, we are asking (pleading?) for God to reach out and help us in our anguish: "I am mourning. I am hurting. I need You to lift me up out of this moment and make me feel whole once again." Say the prayer as much as one wants; I have never seen the vending machine drop a treat down the slot.

Turn the prayer around. Instead of us speaking to God, what if we were to understand these words as God speaking to us. Instead of our voices pleading with God, let the words be God's voice entreating us to see that there is One at our side wanting to lift us up and help us to move forward, One who is there "keeping faith with those who sleep in the dust", who believes in us, and (though there are some who would question how Jewish this sounds, it is very) who loves us, One whose tears are as heavy as ours. Instead of our effort to plead with God, the prayer is a reminder of how much God wants to embrace us.

In our tradition, two of the most common words for prayer are *avodah* and *t'fillah*.

Avodah is understood to mean "sacred service," based on its use as a technical term for the sacrifices of old. Those sacrifices (referred to as *korbanot*, from the root that means to "draw near") were a manner in which our ancestors poured out their hearts to God. That is, their prayer was composed of that which would draw them out of themselves and make room for something greater.

T'fillah is understood to mean "prayer," based on the root that implies judgment, judging oneself.

It is interesting that neither term speaks of asking for anything. They, in essence, ask us to make a little room in our hearts, then look carefully at how we want to fill it up. Yes, if we are full of ourselves there is no room for anything or anyone else. And when understood this way, our prayer experience takes on a very different form and function. The goal is not to ask God for anything as much as it is to listen to and for God's presence in our lives, and from that presence, learn what it is that we have to do to make life what we want it to be.

How much the more so when it comes to mourning. How do you laud God for imploring us to ensure consistency and continuity *l'dor vador*—for generation to generation—when you have a *terminus ad quem* lying in a casket before you?

THE HOLE IN THE HEART THAT MAKES IT WHOLE

When Ricky died, I asked a friend who had lost two siblings how her mother did it. How was this woman able to survive and thrive, having experienced the death of two children. She told me that her mother referred to what she called the hole in her heart. The hole was always there. Sometimes it was smaller. Sometimes it was bigger. But, it was always there.

I shared that story with a colleague in response to the news that his son had died. I did not try to compare our experiences. Nor did I offer any other advice than to share with him that, yes, there is a hole in my heart, but it is that hole that makes me whole. Would I rather have Ricky at my side, alive and thriving? Stupid question! But that he was once at my side makes me who I am, and I would not trade anything in the world for having had that experience and those memories (good and not so good).

I still have some issues with God. Having that hole does not give God a pass. Am I angry with God? My wife thinks so. When the Torah is carried around during the service, unlike the rest of the congregation, I no longer reach out and touch or kiss it. Me and "The Big Guy" have a few issues to work out before we get that cozy again. Yet, I listen for God's voice, especially when I pray. And, since moving to Phoenix and getting involved with a very special congregation, I am reading Torah more than I have in years. And when I read, I use a *yad* (pointer) that was given to Ricky when he became a Bar Mitzvah.

Kind of messy, isn't it? But so is mourning. I am convinced that the rites and rituals of our tradition are essential for mourning.

And I have counseled innumerable people to at least do something, or "it" will come back to bite you in the ____. Mourning is messy. Try as we might to find or create a sense of order out of the chaos, there are times that we cannot. Making the effort to embrace the grief and be embraced by it, to acknowledge that things are going to be a bit different than we planned, to open ourselves up to be aware of the grief and the differences in our lives, is to go beyond the "*mitzvah* mode" of the rites and rituals; it is to allow them to lead us back to life.

It is interesting to me that when driving in my car I have a large windshield in front of me. Yet, I am also surrounded by smaller rear-view mirrors. My vision of the path on which I am traveling is open to all sorts of possibilities. However, unless I continually check on where I am coming from and where I am (figuratively speaking, whether there are cars on my right or on my left) I am not going to get very far. As much as we talk about traffic patterns, we cannot always predict how another driver will behave. We can only control what we do. It takes awareness and intention. So does mourning.

Acknowledging the hole can bring a greater sense of wholeness.

SEEING IS BELIEVING?

The way the Jewish calendar fell this year, Ricky's *yahrtzeit* and the anniversary of his celebrating becoming a Bar Mitzvah were exactly two weeks apart. As his *yahrtzeit* approached, I "knew," though I am not sure why, that it was not going to be easy. And with the Bar Mitzvah date falling as it did, I was preparing myself to enter into my own period of *bein hamitzarim* (literally "between the straights", a term that refers to the three weeks before the 9th of Av, when we remember the destruction of the Temples; a period of time that is mournful and melancholy). I was asked to read Torah the weekend of the *yahrtzeit*, but declined. I was pretty sure that I would not be in the mood. On the Tuesday after I was asked to chant the Haftarah (prophetic reading that accompanies the Torah reading on a Shabbat or holiday). I said yes without thinking. Having chanted and/or taught virtually every Haftarah of the calendar year, I usually do not spend time preparing the reading other than a quick review during the Torah reading, which comes immediately before. This year was pretty much the same. Here it comes!

The Friday night between the *yahrtzeit* and the Bar Mitzvah date there was a knock on our door around 8:30. It was our son, daughter-in-law and granddaughter. Reese handed us a box that Debby had her unwrap and open for us. She presented us with the contents of the box: four cookies that said, "It's A Boy." Alex and Carly are expecting (due in March—poo, poo, poo . . . it should all go well and the baby should be healthy, etc.). It was "the great reveal." Hold that thought.

The next day I almost lost it. I stood up to do the Haftarah. It was from Isaiah. It is one of the seven Haftarot of Comfort with which, after the despair of the 9th of Av, we approach the beginning of the Jewish New Year. And as the text opens, we are taught (Isaiah 51:12): "I, I am He who comforts you!" Or, better: "I am the one who wants to comfort you, is offering comfort to you."

Was that a sign? Was it coincidence? What was I supposed to take from that moment?

Years ago, if someone had come into my office and shared the feeling that they had received a sign, I would have mustered up the most empathic posture I could and hide my skepticism. If it made them feel better, what was the harm? Somewhere along the line, and I cannot put my finger on exactly when, my attitude changed. Maybe I heard too many stories. Maybe I had seen too many moments that had to have been more than coincidence. Now? Now such moments help me make sense out of much more than I ever thought they could.

When a loved one dies, we wonder. Where are they? Can they see us? Will we ever meet them again? Are they OK? When my aunt, who was like a second mother to me, died a couple years ago, as I began the funeral service (which was entirely on Zoom because of COVID—I was not even there), I said something, half kiddingly, to the effect of: "Ricky, you better find a place to hide.

Aunt Jane (who we never told that Ricky had died) is on her way."
Everyone on the Zoom who knew my aunt knew exactly what I
meant and we were able to smile. However, later that day, while
in the back yard, we saw two owls (an owl was Ricky's "totem") in
a tree across the wash watching us. I looked at them, said "Thank
you" and they immediately left. I said "Thank you" because I believed it was a sign that they (Ricky and Aunt Jane) had found each
other and were OK. I found a little piece of peace. Now, the reading
of that Haftarah did the same.

We know that there is little that can make things the way we
want them to be. We want our loved ones back by our side in good
health and good humor. So, what do we do? Do we create a new
normal or do we take that moment to recognize it? Do we open
our hearts and minds to the signs that are all about us that we
might otherwise ignore? Do we pause and acknowledge that God
is with us, at our side, offering us the comfort of His presence?

The greatest power that God exhibits is holding back His
ways and wishes and giving us the room to exercise our free will.
When we mourn, we can choose to focus on the loss or on how
that loss might enable us to ensure that our loved ones remain a
part of us. I have faith that all these little moments that I, and so
many others, experience are more than coincidences. I have faith
that they are trying to tell us something about how to respond to
life as it is lived, not the least of which is to embrace death as part
of life, knowing that we are not alone in grief. God is there to offer
us comfort. And, if we respond to that presence rather than react
to the death, we will find the comfort that we need.

Where is God? How do I know? When people tell me that
they do not believe in God, I usually ask them, "Which one?"
There are images of God that I do not embrace either, especially
when presented as the only understanding that there is. It is not by
accident that our tradition teaches us that God has function but no
form and rejects any attempt to find a form. Yet, that presence can
be felt, and will forever be with us, if we allow it. We can close our
eyes, or we can open them wide and see.

LARRY THE CABLE GUY TAUGHT ME TO BELIEVE

Really! The comedian Larry the Cable Guy has a routine in which, while strumming a guitar, he blurts out the words, "I believe," pauses, and then shares an observation about life that is so absurd, awkward, or actual that one can only laugh. So, while listening to that routine on the radio in my car, I wondered? What do I believe?

I realized, when I started asking that question, that there is a difference between "faith" and "belief." I know I am not the first person to think this way, but it was a bit startling. To me, faith is important because the first step towards having faith in something is to doubt. I have to question. And, I have to question the act of faith as well as the object of my faith, over and over again. However, beliefs lead to surety; they cannot be questioned. Both faith and belief can bring comfort and strength. They can also be challenging and "of concern." My faith is informed by my beliefs. My beliefs are informed by my faith. To have only one without the other would lead me adrift. To have neither would be even worse. The interplay between my faith and my beliefs is at the core of life itself.

Similarly, there is a difference between grief and mourning. Grief is my reaction to loss. Mourning is my response. I grieve the loss of many different things. It is as if pieces of my life have fallen off along the way. How I respond to those missing pieces (handles?) is how I mourn.

I grieve the death of Ricky every day. Sometimes it is with a smile; other times it is with an intense sense of loss. I have my "Ricky moments" on the treadmill, while walking through a store, watching a commercial on television, and especially when I pray (while I am listening to hear what God is trying to say to me). Those moments can be intense and overwhelming. However, more important than any moment is what I do with it. And, the moment I begin to "do with it" is when mourning begins.

To grieve without mourning, or to mourn without such moments of grief, leads me adrift. To do neither would be even worse.

The interplay between grief and mourning is at the foundation of the path that leads to finding the missing handle.

Life is messy. Faith, belief, grief and mourning are, at times, even worse. However, we all have "Larry moments," when we observe life as it is lived, and we have "Ricky moments," when the observation is about us. I bring all of this up because it is my conviction (something in which I believe I will always have faith) that unless we embrace the grief that we experience in life we will never mourn. And if we never mourn, we never learn to appreciate that we have something to grieve. It is hard work. However, unless we do it, life is not (cannot) be lived.

CHARLIE MY CAT GOT RUN OVER BY A CAR. OR, WHY I AM WRITING ANY OF THIS.

For decades, as part of the confirmation class (10th grade) curriculum, I included a unit on Jewish theology. Modern Jews do not do theology well for a number of reasons. However, that did not stop me from trying to teach a little.

After reviewing a number of perspectives on the existence of evil, I handed out a piece of paper with the following, followed by a number of lines:

> Dear God,
>
> Charlie my cat got run over by a car. If you had anything to do with it, you have to tell me why.
>
> Love,
> Harvey

The students were asked to answer Harvey as God (using the perspectives we had studied of Maimonides, Buber and Moses, as well as their own). The answers were profound. And I saved them for years, expecting to put them into some sort of book. Then Ricky died and I realized that I had never answered Harvey myself. What I have written here is what I would have shared with Harvey.

This effort is not meant to be an exercise in emotional or spiritual exhibitionism. Those who know me may be wondering where this came from in the first place. One of my "friends" once asked me if I had "emotional Asperger's" as I never shared much of anything about me with anyone—would not get that close that "we would touch." In fact, it is the opposite. I wrote this, and am sharing it as I am; hoping that those who mourn (which is pretty much every one of us at some time or another) will be able to find meaning when there seems to be none.

No one's grief is better or worse than anyone else's. So many people tell me that losing a child is the worst thing that could ever happen. Well, I disagree. Never having had that child in the first place would be worse. And whether that is a father, mother, sister, brother or spouse, it is the same. When I am hurting, I hurt. How can I begin to move forward? This effort is one suggestion; it is the path that I have been walking along, and continue to stumble down as I try to find my way.

Many years ago, when our oldest son was just a baby, I was visiting with a family from another congregation whose son had just died. I remember standing with the mother when a woman walked up and said: "God must have really loved your son to have taken him back the way he did. You should feel very blessed." The mother looked at me not knowing what to say or do. I got between them and escorted the other woman out of the room (I think I even asked her to leave and come back when she might have something worthwhile to say, and I could have done that because I was already in the process of moving to a new congregation in a different city).

What is the point of that story? It is the point of everything I have written here. We all will someday find ourselves mourning a loss. When we do, or when we see others in pain, we need to understand that we all mourn in our own ways, we will find our grief to be ours and ours alone. And, we will all be confronted with a missing handle. There is no absolute manner in which to find the peace and wholeness that we want and need. However, that handle is out there. And, if we can make room in our hearts . . . discover

55

and cherish the hole that they left behind . . . we will find that our new normal is more than we could ever have imagined.

There is no end to the making of books, especially concerning bereavement, pain, suffering and grief. Why am I sharing these thoughts as I am? What makes this one so different or special? Because it is mine. This is my story. I offer it with the hope and the prayer that because of it (or in spite of it) you will find your story, and find a little piece of peace for yourself, as well.

I do not ask for sympathy. I ask that no hardship fall on anyone. I only ask that when faced with mourning, we find a way to make their memories live, for their sake, if not for ours.

Zichrono l'v'racha: May Ricky have, and be, a blessing

As I have written: the foundation of the journal is a reflection on the moment when, during the course of the funeral, we discovered that the handle needed to lower Ricky into the grave was missing, the actual interment would have to wait. Whether it was forgotten or it was a sign depends on how we look at the world. In retrospect, I sometimes think that any meaning that might be had when life seems utterly bereft of any at all, can be found in exactly such pauses. When we stop and start to look at the world for what it is, take the time to see the bigger picture, allow our hearts and minds to open themselves up to the wonder of life as it is lived, more meaning can be found than in any number of books, or poems or prayers. I found my handle in the pauses between the moments that meant the most. In the quiet, when I opened myself up to see the world not only as it is, but as it was, and as it still can be. The moment that we found the handle to lower Ricky into the ground he was granted his piece of peace. May we each find our missing handles and discover the same for ourselves.

The "Who," "What," "When," "Where" and "How" of a person's death are usually fairly evident. The question of "Why" is what gets us every time.

- *Why is it that not knowing the reasons behind the "Who," "What," "When", "Where" and "How" gives us so much trouble?*

- *Would knowing the "Why" really make that much of a difference?*

- *Is part of our difficulty in accepting the death of a loved one our own sense of guilt (feeling responsible, and that if we had only known we could have done more), which would be assuaged if we knew the "Why?"*

- *How can we find comfort and consolation in face of the "concise ambiguity" which comes from not knowing the "Why".*

- *How can we handle living life with such a hole in our hearts?*

- *How can we start seeing and/or making life meaningful again, for their sake, if not for ours?*